The Inventor's Secret

The Inventor's Secret

What Thomas Edison Told Henry Ford

Suzanne Slade  *Illustrated by* Jennifer Black Reinhardt

Charlesbridge

Thomas Edison

HENRY FORD

With love to my son, Patrick, who always amazes me with his incredible inventions. Keep at it!—**S. S.**

Dedicated with love to my husband, Joe, and my son, Will—my favorite brilliant, curious, and quirky inventors.—**J. B. R.**

Acknowledgments: With special thanks to Alison Giesen, chief curator at the Edison & Ford Winter Estates, and her team; Louis Carlat, PhD, from the Thomas A. Edison Papers at Rutgers University; and the Benson Ford Research Center at the Henry Ford for sharing their invaluable expertise and advice on this project. Thanks also to Leonard DeGraaf at the Thomas Edison National Historical Park for his help with the photographs.

A note to young inventors: Doing experiments, creating inventions, and discovering how things work is exciting. Just remember—safety is the most important part of being an inventor. Be sure to invite an adult or two to watch your invention adventures. (They just might learn something, too!)

Photo credits: Page 42: Thomas Edison National Historical Park, National Park Service, US Department of the Interior • Page 43: Library of Congress, LC-USZ62-62268 • Page 44: Library of Congress, LC-USZ62-21222

Text copyright © 2015 by Suzanne Slade
Illustrations copyright © 2015 by Jennifer Black Reinhardt
All rights reserved, including the right of reproduction in whole or in part in any form. Charlesbridge and colophon are registered trademarks of Charlesbridge Publishing, Inc.

Published by Charlesbridge, 85 Main Street, Watertown, MA 02472
(617) 926-0329 • www.charlesbridge.com

Illustrations done in watercolor, ink, and black colored pencil on
    Arches bright white 300-lb. hot-press watercolor paper
Display type set in Bootstrap by Aerotype
Text type set in Arno Pro by Adobe
Color separations by Colourscan Print Co Pte Ltd, Singapore
Printed by 1010 Printing International Limited
    in Huizhou, Guangdong, China
Production supervision by Brian G. Walker
Designed by Whitney Leader-Picone

Library of Congress Cataloging-in-Publication Data
Slade, Suzanne, author.
    The Inventor's secret: what Thomas Edison told Henry Ford /
Suzanne Slade; illustrated by Jennifer Black Reinhardt.
        pages cm
    Includes bibliographical references.
    ISBN 978-1-58089-667-2 (reinforced for library use)
    ISBN 978-1-60734-763-7 (ebook)
    ISBN 978-1-60734-712-5 (ebook pdf)
1. Edison, Thomas A. (Thomas Alva), 1847–1931—Juvenile literature.
2. Ford, Henry, 1863–1947—Juvenile literature. 3. Inventors—United
States—Biography—Juvenile literature. 4. Scientists—United States—
Biography—Juvenile literature. I. Reinhardt, Jennifer Black, 1963–
illustrator. II. Title.

T39.S56 2015
609.2'273—dc23   2014010494

Printed in China
(hc) 10 9 8 7 6 5 4 3 2 1

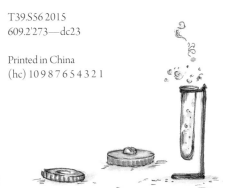

Not so long ago the world was a little slower. A little simpler. And a whole lot quieter.

No airplanes roaring overhead. No cars rumbling down roads. No phones ringing in pockets.

Then things began to change—because of two curious boys, Thomas and Henry.

And one secret.

Young Thomas got into trouble. A lot.

It always started with an "experiment." He just had to see how things worked.

Thomas was curious about chemistry. He mixed up colorful potions in his basement, but explosions shook the house night and day.

Thomas was curious about locomotives. He got a job as a newsboy, selling papers on a train, but one of his experiments set the baggage car on fire.

Home sweet home

Most of all, Thomas was curious about electricity—invisible energy that flowed and stopped, sizzled and popped. He tied wires to his cats' tails and rubbed their fur. Sparks flew that day!

Henry was born sixteen years after Thomas. He got in a heap of trouble, too. He was always doing experiments instead of his chores. He just had to see how things worked.

Henry was curious about windup toys. He took his sister's toys apart, but couldn't always get them back together.

Henry was curious about the rushing river. He built a dam and waterwheel to catch its energy, but flooded the neighbor's field instead.

Most of all, Henry was curious about engines—machines
that chugged and purred, hiccupped and whirred. He built
a steam engine from a ten-gallon can, tin blades, and a pipe.
But it exploded and set the school fence on fire!

As Thomas grew older he dreamed of creating his own inventions—electric gadgets to make life easier. He designed an electric pen so people could rest their weary hands. His sharp pen cut a stencil that made copies. In just one day people could print a pile of copies that would've taken weeks to write by hand.

As Henry grew older he dreamed of creating his own inventions, too—powerful engines to make life easier. When he was twelve he spied something amazing—an engine-powered buggy. He'd never seen a vehicle that wasn't pulled by a horse.

Henry sprinted up to the buggy, his mind filled with questions. What powered the engine? How fast did it go? What could it do?

The driver boasted the vehicle ran on coal and steam. It went about twelve miles an hour. Its engine powered farm equipment and huge saws.

The mighty machine got Henry's mind spinning.

An engine didn't eat or rest like a horse. It could carry people, mail, and news. Fast!

From then on, Henry thought about one thing: making his own vehicle. A car hardworking families could afford. Then folks could go to town anytime, not just the weekly Saturday trip. They could visit faraway places they'd only heard about.

14

But Henry couldn't even repair his broken watch! How would he ever build a car?

Then he heard about Thomas's electric pen.

What's his secret? Henry wondered. *How did he make such a marvelous machine?*

Later, Thomas created an invention that recorded and played back sounds. When Thomas talked into his new phonograph: "Mary had a little lamb," it talked right back: "Mary had a little lamb." His phonograph could also play music.

Henry was still dreaming about cars. Everywhere he went, his pockets rattled with metal parts. When he was seventeen he took a job at a machine shop to learn more about engines and machinery. Two years later a farmer hired Henry to operate a new steam engine.

Soon Henry began tinkering on a steam engine of his own.
He strapped the homemade engine to an old mowing machine.
His contraption sputtered along for forty feet, then collapsed.

Henry's design was a flop!

But everyone was buzzing about Thomas's talking phonograph.

What's his secret? Henry wondered.

Meanwhile, Thomas was working on an electric light so people could read past dark. After changing his design many times, he created an incandescent lightbulb that burned all night!

Henry was determined to make his vehicle work, so he took a job at a company that made engines. One day he repaired a fancy engine from England. It had a four-stroke cylinder that burned gas to create power. Fascinated, he built a model of the engine to see how it worked.

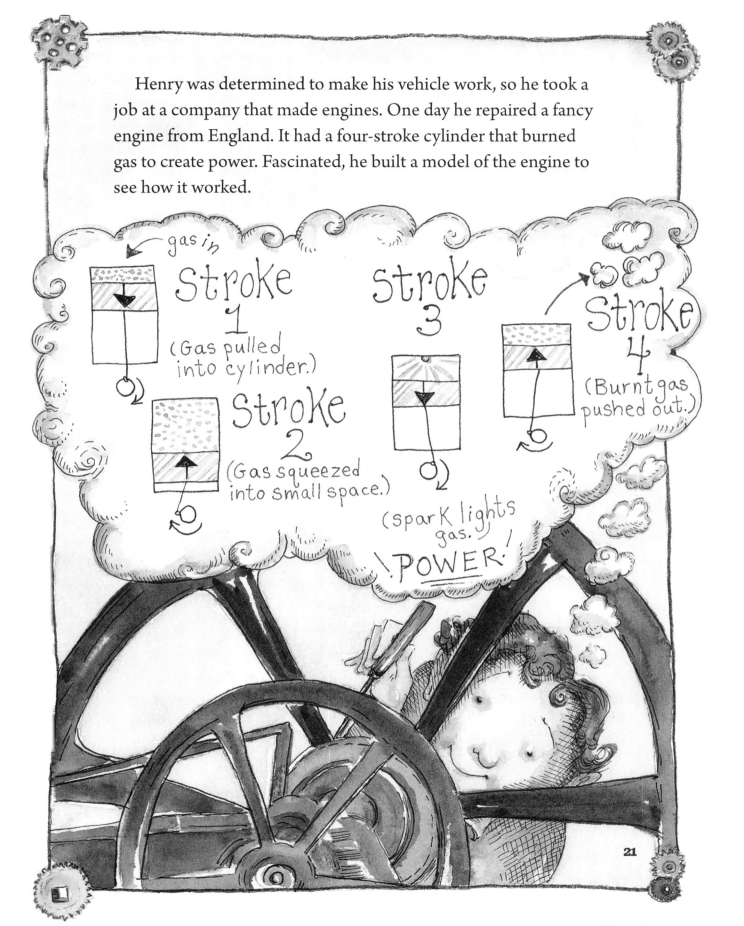

gas in

Stroke 1
(Gas pulled into cylinder.)

Stroke 2
(Gas squeezed into small space.)

Stroke 3
(spark lights gas. !POWER!)

Stroke 4
(Burnt gas pushed out.)

After that, Henry spent long nights, and Saturdays, working on his car. Friends and coworkers helped, too. When he finally rolled his creation out of his workshop, it had two cylinders for double the power, a three-gallon tank for gas, and four bicycle tires for wheels.

Henry's Quadricycle could go up to twenty miles per hour— but it cost a fortune to make. Most people thought his rattling gas buggy was a joke.

"Get a horse!" people shouted at Henry.

But the whole country was crazy about Thomas's
electric light.

Henry scratched his head. *What's his secret?*

Still, Henry believed in his dream. Although he knew that other people were working on gas cars, he was determined to make the best. One that was easy to drive. Big enough for families. And most important—a car everyone could afford.

While Henry was working on his design, Thomas earned patents for over one hundred new inventions.

Henry couldn't stand it any longer.

He had to find out Thomas's secret!

So Henry hopped a train in Detroit and chugged six hundred miles to New York City. That's where important businessmen, including Thomas, were gathering for a meeting.

Henry did some fast talking and got invited to a big dinner with Thomas as the guest of honor.

During dinner, everyone kept talking to Thomas.

Henry peered down the large table at the famous inventor.

He waited.

And waited.

And waited.

Finally Henry gathered his courage. He moved right next to Thomas and told him he was building a gas car.

"Is it a four-cycle engine?" Thomas asked.

Henry lit up brighter than any lightbulb. He grabbed a menu and started sketching his engine.

Thomas fired off question after question.

Henry happily answered each one.

And that's when it happened.
Blue eyes sparkling, Thomas leaned in close to Henry.
He banged his fist on the table. "Keep at it!" he shouted.

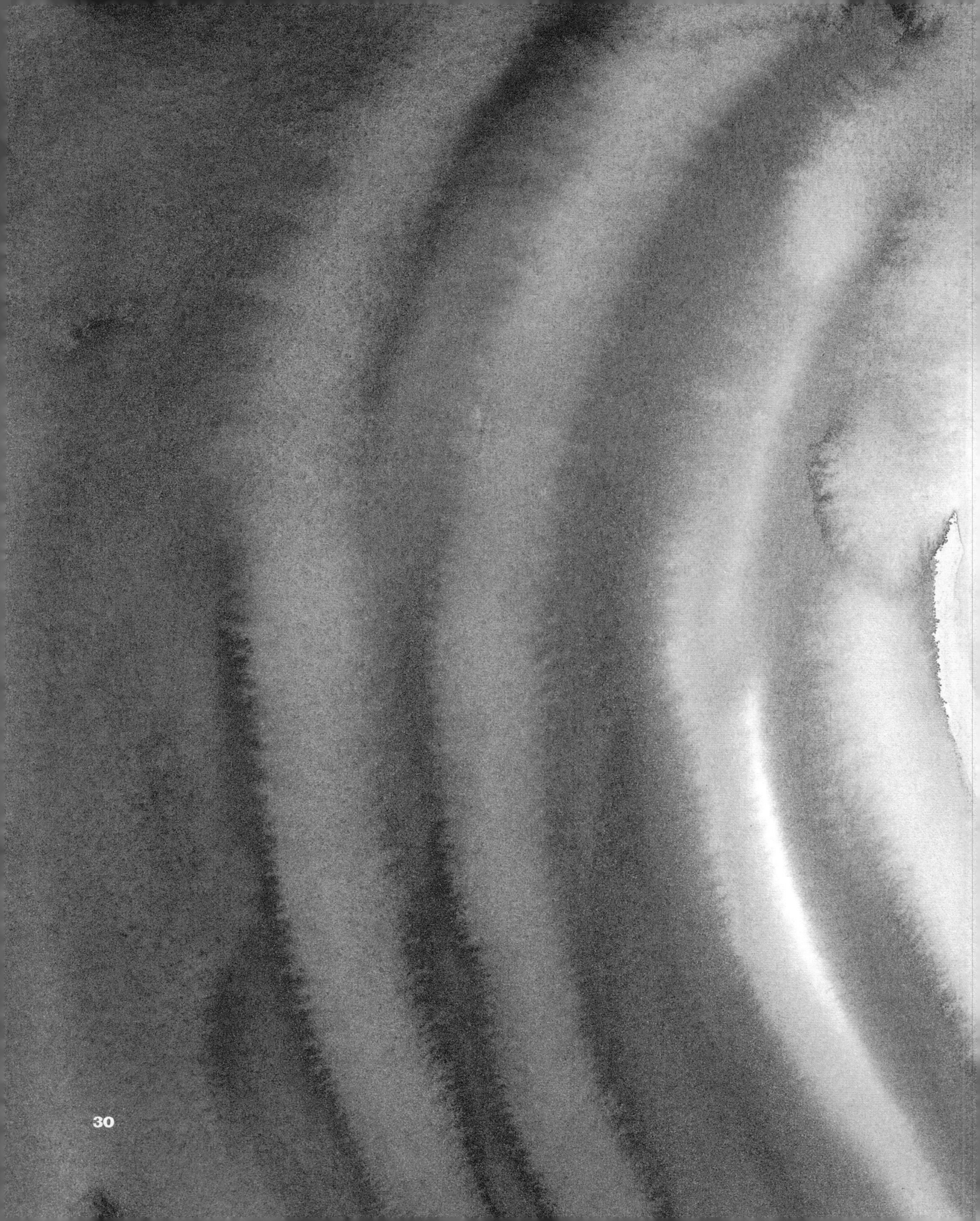

Henry smiled.
Keep at it?
Henry laughed.
He'd known Thomas's secret all along!

So Henry kept at it. Year after year.

He made a car named the Model A. But it cost too much for most hardworking folks.

The Model A

1903

Two cylinders

Two seats

Too expensive

He kept at it and made the Model B. Still too expensive.

THE MODEL B

↑ Four cylinders
Four seats
Even *more* expensive!

Models C, F, K, and N weren't quite right either.

Henry grew tired.

How many letters would it take?

Model C

Bigger gas tank
Extra foot room
Costs too much

Model F

Five passengers
Still too much money

Then he remembered. Thomas had changed his lightbulb design thousands of times before he got it right.
So Henry kept at it.

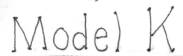

Model K

Model N

Powerful engine
— six cylinders
But too heavy
— 1,800 pounds
And too expensive!

Lighter weight,
but too small
Bumpy ride, but
a good price!

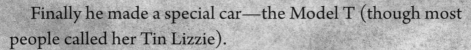

Finally he made a special car—the Model T (though most people called her Tin Lizzie).

Lizzie was light, fast, and had four powerful cylinders. She didn't have fancy extras like a driver door, gas gauge, seat belts, or shocks, but she had plenty of room for a family. Millions of people bought their own Tin Lizzies. She took folks to town whenever they wanted. She carried people places they'd never been. Best of all, she brought people across the country closer together.

Things had changed. The world was a little faster and a whole lot more exciting.

And it was all because of two curious inventors, Thomas and Henry, and one secret . . .

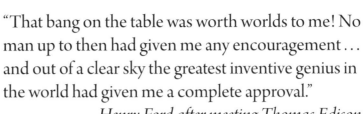

"That bang on the table was worth worlds to me! No man up to then had given me any encouragement ... and out of a clear sky the greatest inventive genius in the world had given me a complete approval."
—*Henry Ford after meeting Thomas Edison*

A Special Friendship

Henry Ford learned Thomas Edison's secret in 1896. After that, the two became very close friends—and they remained friends for over thirty years! Grateful for the older inventor's encouraging words, Henry gave Thomas a shiny new Model T in 1916. Henry tried to give Thomas a new car every year after that, but each time Thomas said no, because the car he had worked just fine.

Thomas and Henry went on camping trips to get away from their busy schedules, although nosy photographers usually followed them wherever they went. Sometimes other famous friends, such as tire businessman Harvey Firestone, naturalist John Burroughs, and even President Warren Harding, came along, too. On their trips Thomas and Henry chatted about chemistry and engineering. They also enjoyed figuring out how much power was created by the old mills they found along the way.

Thomas spent his winters in Fort Meyers, Florida. Eventually Henry bought the house right next to him. The two friends installed a gate (later nicknamed the "friendship gate") in the fence between their yards, so they could visit each other whenever they wanted.

Author's Note

For nonfiction authors a new story often begins with a fascinating, little-known fact that sparks a magical "goose-bump" moment. When I learned Thomas Edison, one of the greatest inventors of all time, pounded his fist on the table and shouted, "Keep at it!" to Henry Ford, that was one of those moments for me.

As I wove the stories of Henry and Thomas together, it was difficult to determine the exact time some of their projects were officially "invented," so I turned to patent records and experts. For example, Thomas had more than one hundred patents relating to his incandescent electric light. Its success didn't depend on a single invention, but on all its parts working together. With assistance from the Thomas A. Edison Papers, I discovered that Thomas's first real breakthrough, a carbon filament, was in October 1879 (US Patent 223,898). Thousands of experiments later, he finally had a commercially useful bulb—one that burned through the night—by the end of 1881 (although it wasn't available for most homes until years later).

As an engineer and an author of historical books, I find it fascinating to see how new inventions have changed lives through the years. For example, in 1900 my great-grandfather Dr. Charles Thomas was a "horse and buggy doc" who had to depend on his horse to get to patients' homes. In 1907 Doc Thomas "went modern" and bought Henry's Model R so he would have faster, more reliable transportation to patients in need. Henry's car helped my great-grandfather arrive in time to deliver more than one thousand babies.

Illustrator's Note

While working on this book, I spent days trying to discover what Henry's first vehicle looked like. I knew that Henry had attached his engine to an "old mower." But there were several types of mowers in the 1800s. Did it have three wheels or four? How did Henry mount a steam engine onto it, and what did that engine look like? When I described my problem to an author friend, she said, "I never thought of that. We write the words about something—you have to show it and draw it!"

Having to "show it and draw it" led me down many fascinating paths on this project. My favorite involved a disappearing mustache. Later in life Henry hired an artist to paint a picture of Henry meeting Thomas at the dinner in New York. As I studied the picture, I made an interesting discovery: Henry has no mustache in the painting—but in photographs from that exact time, he did have one! Henry grew his mustache sometime between 1889 and 1892, so I've included it in all the illustrations from the Quadricycle on.

Learning about something so you can draw it—that's the job of an illustrator. But it's also my job to make artistic judgment calls. To avoid confusion, I've painted Henry with a mustache at the end of the book—even though he shaved it off in 1902.

Details About Inventions

Young Thomas and Henry tinkered in basements, workshops, and even train cars to find out how things worked. As adults they worked in well-equipped laboratories with engineers, machinists, chemists, and electricians to create their new inventions. Here are a few more details about the inventions in the story.

Thomas's Electric Pen

Priced at thirty dollars, Thomas's electric pen was a big seller in 1875. The pen had a sharp point that moved up and down quickly. As the pen traced over the lines of a document to be copied, its tip cut hundreds of tiny holes and created a stencil. To make a copy, ink was pressed through the holes of the stencil onto another piece of paper.

Thomas's Phonograph

In 1877 Thomas turned the crank on his tinfoil phonograph and said, "Mary had a little lamb." The sound waves of his voice vibrated a flexible diaphragm inside, which caused a needle to vibrate. The vibrating needle scratched small dents in a piece of tinfoil wrapped around a cylinder. After adjusting the machine to play back sounds, Thomas turned the crank again. The scratches on the tinfoil made the needle vibrate, causing the diaphragm to vibrate and reproduce his voice.

Thomas's Incandescent Electric Light

The electric light, or lightbulb as we call it today, is Thomas's most famous invention. A metal socket on a glass bulb held a thin filament inside. Electricity heated the filament until it glowed. Thomas's biggest challenge was finding a filament that would glow a long time and not burn up or melt. After testing boxwood, hickory, cedar, and thousands of other materials, he finally chose a carbonized bamboo filament for his commercial lightbulb.

Henry's Early Cars and the Model T

Henry Ford wasn't the first to build a gas-powered car, but he dreamed of creating an affordable, reliable vehicle that was big enough for a family. Most of Henry's early cars were considered "successful," but he finally realized his dream of a large, low-cost car with the Model T.

In 1903 Henry partnered with investors to start the Ford Motor Company. His first production car, the Model A (shown here), had two cylinders and cost $750. A two-seater, it was too small for families, unless you paid another $100 for a backseat. The Model A sold fairly well, but the car was heavy and had reliability issues.

While Henry hoped to create an inexpensive car, his company directors believed that a high-priced luxury car would produce bigger profits, so a larger Model B with polished wood and brass trim came out in 1904. This four-passenger, four-cylinder car was priced at $2,000. Models C and F, updated versions of the Model A, also released in 1904. The Model C had two cylinders, seated two passengers, and cost $800. A backseat ran another $100. The Model F, priced at $1,000, had room for five.

When investors asked for more luxury cars, the company produced the Model K, a grand-touring car with six cylinders. It cost a whopping $2,800, and Henry lost money on each car. His next production car, the Model N, was made with a new, strong, lightweight metal called vanadium steel. This car cost $450, but it was a two-seater—too small for a family. The Model N sold well despite its small size and terribly bumpy ride, but Henry still dreamed of a bigger, reasonably priced car. He revised the Model N to create Models R and S, both lightweight two-seaters, but his major breakthrough came with the next letter, T.

Henry shared his dream for the Model T in 1907: "I will build a motor car for the great multitude. It will be large enough for the family, but small enough for the individual to run and care for. . . . But it will be so low in price that no man making a good salary will be unable to own one." Henry achieved his goals with the help of vanadium steel and brand-new part designs by his engineering team.

When the Model T (shown below) debuted in 1908 at a cost of $850, it wasn't the lowest-priced car on the market. But its unique suspension with high axles allowed it to easily roll over huge potholes, muddy roads, and snowdrifts. To farmers the Model T was more than transportation; it was a helping hand. By jacking the car up and removing one tire, farmers could use its powerful spinning wheel to help pump water, press cider, or saw wood.

In its first year, 10,660 Model Ts were built. As production later increased, its price dropped. In 1913 Henry introduced the moving assembly line, in which parts were moved past workers who stood in one place and performed only one task. The new line shortened the assembly time for each car, which meant more cars could be built. That year, 189,000 Model Ts rolled off the line, and the cost dropped to $550. In 1914 Henry raised his workers' daily wage from $2.34 to $5 per day. The higher pay reduced worker turnover, which saved more time and money. The next year the price of a Model T fell to $440. By 1926 it was $260, less than one-third of its original price.

While its low cost was key, the Model T was also popular because people could fix it themselves. All they needed were inexpensive parts from the local hardware store. And "Tin Lizzie" was always ready to help out—with a trip to town, a vacation, or farm chores. It's no surprise owners thought of Lizzie as part of the family!

Source Notes

Please note: While it's impossible to know Henry's exact thoughts, we know he considered Thomas "the greatest man in the world" before they ever met (My Friend Mr. Edison, page 9). Based on this, the author has depicted the young, ambitious Henry wondering about the famous inventor's secret to success throughout the book. For more information about the sources below, see the selected bibliography on page 48.

pp. 6–7: Thomas had chemical lab in basement, sold newspapers on train, set baggage car on fire: Israel, pp. 11, 12, 17, 18. He tested electricity with cats: Dyer and Martin, pp. 48, 49.

pp. 8–9: Henry disliked farm chores, loved machinery: Ford, *My Life and Work*, p. 24. He took sister's toys apart, built dam and steam engine: Watts, pp. 7, 8, 15.

pp. 10–11: Electric pen (1875) details: Israel, p. 106.

pp. 12–13: Henry saw his "first vehicle other than horse-drawn" at age twelve (1875). It ran on coal and steam, drove threshing machines and sawmills, and went twelve miles an hour (speed from Henry's comparison to a similar engine in 1879): Ford, *My Life and Work*, pp. 22–25.

pp. 14–15: Henry received first watch at age twelve (1875) but couldn't repair it. He first repaired a watch at age thirteen (1876): Ford, *My Life and Work*, pp. 22, 23.

p. 16: Thomas recorded and played back "Mary Had a Little Lamb" on phonograph (1877): "Tinfoil Phonograph."

p. 17: Henry carried nuts, washers, and machinery parts in his pockets. He became a machine shop apprentice at Dry Dock Engine Works (1880): Ford, *My Life and Work*, pp. 23, 24. He moved home and operated new steam engine for neighbor (1882): Watts, pp. 26, 27.

pp. 18–19: Henry built steam-powered vehicle, which broke after forty feet: Watts, pp. 26, 27.

p. 20: Thomas changed incandescent light design many times: Iles, p. 135. He invented incandescent light that burned all night: "T. A. Edison Electric-Lamp."

p. 21: Henry repaired single-cylinder Otto engine (1885), built a model of engine (1887): Ford, *My Life and Work*, p. 28.

p. 22: Henry's Quadricycle had two cylinders, a three-gallon gas tank, twenty-eight-inch bicycle tires, and a top speed of twenty miles per hour: Ford, *My Life and Work*, pp. 30, 31. Quadricycle made first trip on Detroit streets on June 4, 1896: Watts, p. 40. "Get a horse!": Bak, p. 26.

pp. 24–25: Henry wanted to create an easy-to-drive, affordable family car: Bak, p. 54. From 1887 (when Henry built four-stroke engine model) to August 1896 (when Henry and Thomas met), Thomas was issued more than one hundred US patents: "Edison's Patents."

p. 26: Henry met Thomas at Association of Edison Illuminating Companies convention in New York City (August 1896). Thomas sat at head of oval table: Ford and Crowther, *My Friend Mr. Edison*, p. 5; Watts, p. 41.

p. 28: Thomas asked, "Is it a four-cycle engine?": Ford and Crowther, *My Friend Mr. Edison*, p. 7; Henry drew sketches on menu: Watts, p. 42.

p. 29: Thomas banged his fist on table and said, "Keep at it!" [exclamation point added]: Ford and Crowther, *My Friend Mr. Edison*, p. 8; Watts, p. 42.

pp. 32–33: Model A facts: Brinkley, p. 66. Model B facts: Lacey, p. 77.

pp. 34–35: Models C, F, K, and N facts: Lacey, pp. 77–90; Brinkley, pp. 68–70, 88.

Thomas's team tested at least six thousand plants in search of a filament: Iles, p. 135.

p. 37: Model T, nicknamed "Tin Lizzie," had four cylinders but no driver door, gas gauge, or shock absorbers: Bak, pp. 54, 55, 59. Model T was light, held four adults. Millions owned Model Ts: Casey and Dodge, pp. 4, 7, 9. Model T took people places they'd never been: Lacey, pp. 96, 97.

p. 40: "That bang … approval": Ford and Crowther, *My Friend Mr. Edison*, p. 8. Thomas received Model T but declined future cars: Stross, p. 242; Alison Giesen (Edison & Ford Winter Estates). Thomas and Henry went on camping trips together; they were joined by Firestone, Burroughs, Harding, and others: Stross, pp. 254, 256; Bak, p. 185. Thomas and Henry discussed chemistry, engineering, and mill power: Burroughs, sequence 45; Lacey, p. 204. Thomas had home in Fort Myers, FL. Henry bought house next door: "Fort Myers Timeline." "Friendship gate" facts: Smoot, pp. 216 , 265–66.

p. 41: Incandescent electric light facts: "Electric Light and Power Patents"; Louis Carlat (the Thomas A. Edison Papers). Mustache dates: Olson, pp. 54, 56.

p. 42: Electric pen facts: "Electric Pen"; Israel p. 107. Phonograph facts: "Tinfoil Phonograph." Incandescent electric light facts: Iles, p. 135; "T. A. Edison Electric-Lamp" and "Electric Lamp"; Louis Carlat (the Thomas A. Edison Papers).

pp. 43–44: Models A, B, C, F, K, N, R, and S facts: Brinkley, pp. 58, 66–70, 88, 100–101; Lacey, pp. 76–78, 89–91. Model T facts: Bak, pp. 54–56, 59; Brinkley, pp. 100, 101, 111, 118; Lacey, pp. 94, 96, 117; Watts, p. 135. "I will … own one": Lacey, p. 87.

The Life of Thomas Edison

 1847: Thomas Edison born in Milan, Ohio.

 1857: Thomas sets up a lab in his basement.

 1862: Thomas works for the Grand Trunk Railroad and sets a baggage car on fire.

 1863: Thomas begins working as a telegrapher.

 1869: Thomas awarded a patent for his "electric vote-recorder" (the first of his 1,093 US patents).

 1875: Thomas develops electric pen (patented in 1876).

 1877: Thomas invents phonograph at his laboratory in Menlo Park, New Jersey.

 1879: Thomas makes a breakthrough on incandescent electric light with a carbon filament that burns through the night (US Patent 223,898 issued in 1880).

 1881: Thomas's electric light is available for commercial use.

 1887: Thomas opens a new laboratory in West Orange, New Jersey.

1891: Thomas and his team apply for patents for the Kinetograph, a motion-picture camera, and the Kinetoscope, a motion-picture viewer.

 1863: Henry Ford born near Dearborn, Michigan.

1875: Henry sees first road engine at age 12.

1893: Henry builds his first gasoline engine. He calls it the "kitchen sink engine" after he clamps it to his kitchen sink and fires it up on Christmas Eve.

 1887: Henry builds his own model of the Otto engine.

 1885: Henry repairs a four-stroke Otto engine from England, which runs on coal-gas used for lighting.

 1882: Henry creates his first "vehicle" from a homemade engine and an old mower.

 1880: Henry works as a machine shop apprentice at Dry Dock Engine Works in Detroit.

The Life of Henry Ford

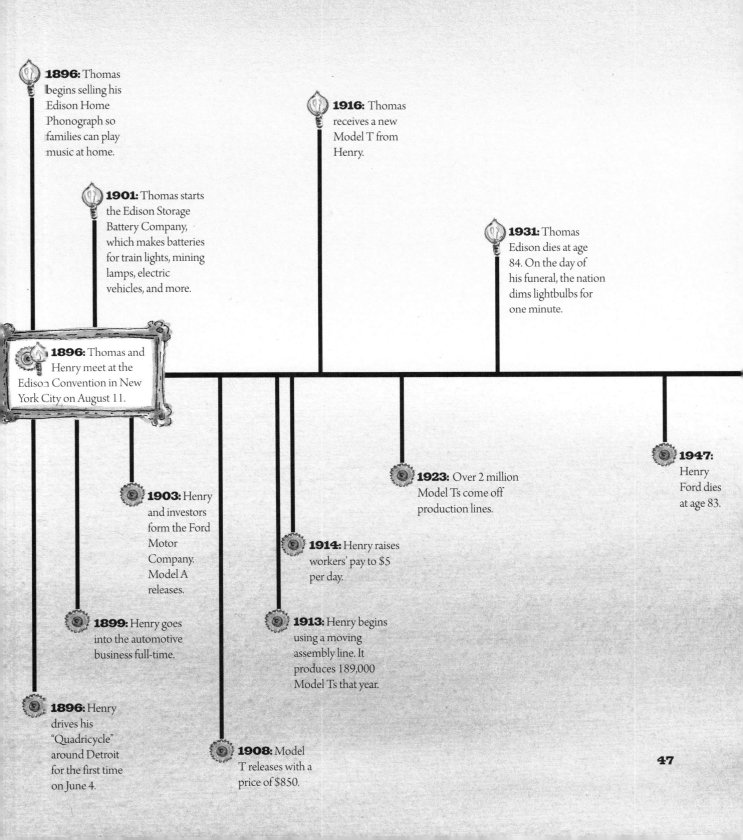

1896: Thomas begins selling his Edison Home Phonograph so families can play music at home.

1916: Thomas receives a new Model T from Henry.

1901: Thomas starts the Edison Storage Battery Company, which makes batteries for train lights, mining lamps, electric vehicles, and more.

1931: Thomas Edison dies at age 84. On the day of his funeral, the nation dims lightbulbs for one minute.

1896: Thomas and Henry meet at the Edison Convention in New York City on August 11.

1903: Henry and investors form the Ford Motor Company. Model A releases.

1923: Over 2 million Model Ts come off production lines.

1947: Henry Ford dies at age 83.

1914: Henry raises workers' pay to $5 per day.

1899: Henry goes into the automotive business full-time.

1913: Henry begins using a moving assembly line. It produces 189,000 Model Ts that year.

1896: Henry drives his "Quadricycle" around Detroit for the first time on June 4.

1908: Model T releases with a price of $850.

Selected Bibliography

Websites

"Fort Myers Timeline," Edison & Ford Winter Estates
    http://www.edisonfordwinterestates.org/collections/biographies/fort-myers/

The Thomas A. Edison Papers, Rutgers University
    "Edison's Patents": http://edison.rutgers.edu/patents.htm
    "Electric Lamp": http://edison.rutgers.edu/lamp.htm
    "Electric Light and Power Patents": http://edison.rutgers.edu/elecpats.htm
    "Electric Pen": http://edison.rutgers.edu/pen.htm
    "T. A. Edison Electric-Lamp": http://edison.rutgers.edu/patents/00223898.PDF
    "Tinfoil Phonograph": http://edison.rutgers.edu/tinfoil.htm

Books

Bak, Richard. *Henry and Edsel: The Creation of the Ford Empire*. Hoboken, NJ: John Wiley & Sons, 2003.

Burroughs, John. *Our Vacation Days of 1918*. Accessed through the Harvard University Library Page Delivery Service.
    http://nrs.harvard.edu/urn-3:FHCL:10870861

Brinkley, Douglas. *Wheels for the World: Henry Ford, His Company, and a Century of Progress*. New York: Viking, 2003.

Casey, Bob, John Dodge, and Horace Dodge. *Henry Ford and Innovation*. Dearborn, MI: The Henry Ford, 2010.
    http://www.thehenryford.org/education/erb/HenryFordAndInnovation.pdf

Dyer, Frank Lewis, and Thomas Commerford Martin. *Edison: His Life and Inventions*. Vol. 1. New York: Harper & Brothers, 1929.

Ford, Henry, with Samuel Crowther. *My Life and Work*. Garden City, NY: Doubleday, Page & Co., 1922.

Ford, Henry, and Samuel Crowther. *My Friend Mr. Edison*. London: Ernest Benn, 1930. Reprint, Whitefish, MT: Kessinger, 2003. Page references are to the 2003 edition.

Iles, George, ed. *Little Masterpieces of Autobiography*. Vol. 3, *Men of Science*. New York: Doubleday, Page & Co., 1908. Accessed through Google Books. http://bit.ly/16yOA7O

Israel, Paul. *Edison: A Life of Invention*. New York: John Wiley & Sons, 1998.

Lacey, Robert. *Ford: The Men and the Machine*. Boston: Little, Brown, 1986.

Olson, Sidney. *Young Henry Ford: A Picture History of the First Forty Years*. Detroit, MI: Wayne State University Press, 1963. Reprint, 1997.

Smoot, Tom. *The Edisons of Fort Myers*. Sarasota, FL: Pineapple Press, 2004.

Stross, Randall. *The Wizard of Menlo Park: How Thomas Alva Edison Invented the Modern World*. New York: Crown Publishers, 2007.

Watts, Steven. *The People's Tycoon: Henry Ford and the American Century*. New York: Knopf, 2005.